MW00902700

Hidden Treasure

Amazing Stories of Discovery

Annick Press Ltd
Toronto • New York • Vancouver

by Tina
Holdcroft
Tina has sailed
across the Atlantic four times,
dodged whales, survived storms,
and anchored in the
harbors of 23 countries.

Design: Sheryl Shapiro

Annick Press Ltd.

We acknowledge the support of the Canada Council for the Arts, the Ontario Arts Council, the Government of Ontario through the Ontario Book Publishers Tax Credit program and the Ontario Book Initiative, and the Government of Canada through the Book Publishing Industry Development Program (BPIDP) for our publishing activities.

Cataloging in Publication

Holdcroft, Tina
Hidden treasure : amazing stories of discovery / written and illustrated by Tina Holdcroft.

(Hidden!)
Includes bibliographical references and index.
ISBN 1-55037-803-1 (bound).–ISBN 1-55037-802-3 (pbk.)

1. Archaeology–Juvenile literature. 2. Treasure-trove–Juvenile literature. I. Title. II. Series: Hidden! (Toronto, Ont.)

CC171.H64 2003 j930.1 C2003-901333-2

The art in this book was rendered in watercolor.
The text was typeset in Clearface, Officina, and Smile.

Distributed in Canada by:
Firefly Books Ltd.
3680 Victoria Park Avenue
Willowdale, ON
M2H 3K1

Published in the U.S.A. by Annick Press (U.S.) Ltd.
Distributed in the U.S.A. by:
Firefly Books (U.S.) Inc.
P.O. Box 1338
Ellicott Station
Buffalo, NY 14205

Manufactured in China.

Visit us at: www.annickpress.com

for Keith Morgan, my friend and husband, who I have totally ignored while working on this book.

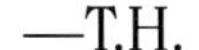
—T.H.

Contents

Introduction

What's shiny, old, rare, and beautiful? It's probably treasure and it could be buried right under your feet!

No! Put that shovel down! The author and publisher do not wish to be responsible for you digging up Auntie's flower bed and smashing through a sewer pipe. Instead, dig into the pages of this book and uncover a fantastic trove of hidden treasure and amazing stories of discovery! (Psst! Hunt up some really useful treasure tips too!)

Treasure Tips

Why do treasure hunters search the beach after a storm? How can you tell the difference between gold and fool's gold? What's an artifact?

Find out what the experts know. Dig into this trove of treasure tips and fascinating facts. Who knows, one day this information might be very useful!

These treasure tips are brilliant!

Ooof!

Where do you look for treasure? The local library is a great place to start. See how the clues in a book lead to incredible treasure on page 18.

TREASURE MAPS FOR SALE! Don't trust that treasure map. Why would you sell a real treasure map when you could find the fortune yourself?

Ooof!

How old is that golden helmet? Ask the skull wearing it! Organic things like bone or wood contain a tiny time clock called carbon 14.

This element starts to decay when the tree is cut, the person dies or the cotton is picked from the plant. Scientists read the carbon 14 time clock by calculating its rate of decay. This helmet is 2,000 years old!

It's easy to tell the age of a metal coin when it has the date stamped right on it!

The surface of silver turns black over time, but gold shines bright forever!

You can dig a million holes and never find treasure. It's much easier to go for a walk with a metal detector. This device, invented in the mid 20th century, can locate buried metal objects from pop-can lids to coins and cannons!

Silver treasure!
Candy wrapper.
What's that strange object in the sea?
Australia.
A bird's-eye view from an airplane can spot ancient Roman roads and remote ruins. Why is there a strange mound in the middle of that flat field?
Why do treasure hunters search a beach after a storm? Strong winds and waves can pull sunken treasure and artifacts ashore, as well as uncover buried beach treasure.
Don't be fooled by fool's gold! Pyrite is yellow and shiny just like gold, but it's worthless. How can you tell the difference? Try the crush test! Gold will dent and bend. Pyrite is made of tiny crystals that crumble under pressure.
Artifacts are man-made objects like clay pots and tools. They are not nearly as rare or valuable as treasure, but they tell a lot about how people lived.
Know the difference. Treasure hunters dig for one reason. To find treasure! Archeologists dig to learn about people and events of the past. Of course, they are always delighted to find treasure too!
Don't hold your breath! Since SCUBA diving equipment was invented in the mid 1900s, divers can breathe easy as they search for sunken treasure.
Where's the treasure chest? Wood decays and iron fastenings rust away in damp hiding places, but survive for centuries in super-dry places.
Did you know that it's a grave mistake to dig up burial grounds? Check out page 28 for more treasure hunting do's and don'ts

Tutankhamun's Tomb

Howard Carter knows that this is his last chance to find the tomb of Tutankhamun, in Egypt's Valley of the Kings. Lord Carnarvon, who has paid for Carter's archeology for many years, has grown tired of Egypt and Carter's empty holes in the sand. The money will dry up at the end of the season and so will Carter's dreams unless he discovers something really big.

With no time to lose, the worried Carter makes the decision to dig under the ruins of some ancient huts. Amazingly, when the first hut is pulled down, the workmen uncover the beginnings of a staircase!

While digging out the sand and rubble, a plaster and brick doorway emerges. It is inscribed with a jackal head, the Egyptian god of the dead. Carter is thrilled, for he knows he has found a royal tomb. Lord Carnarvon quickly arrives from England.

Sixteen steps are cleared and the plaster and brick doorway is opened. Beyond lies a long passageway filled with rubble and this too is cleared. Now Howard Carter stands before the final door.

On November 26, 1922, he drills a hole, inserts a candle, then peers inside.

Tut's treasure is truly amazing! Now, take a deep breath and read. Six full-sized chariots, hundreds of royal statues, boats, golden daggers and alabaster jars, a throne and chairs, beds and game boards, and ornate chests full of clothes, and incredible jewelry. Wait—there's more!
Blow out that candle. I'm trying to sleep.
Tut's mummy, with its fantastic death mask, is inside three nesting mummy cases. The inner one is made of 1,088 kilograms (2,400 pounds) of solid gold. And there's more!
Breathtaking! If this leaves you gasping for air, imagine how Carter felt.

Many royal tombs are carved into the rock of the Valley of the Kings. By 1000 BCE (that's just over 3,000 years ago) almost all of these tombs had lost their treasures to thieves.
Tutankhamun was only nine years old when he became Pharaoh of Egypt over 3,300 years ago. But the "boy king" never really ruled, as all decisions were made by a group of powerful men. Strangely enough, just as Tut was ready to take over, he mysteriously died at the age of eighteen.
I wonder how he got that wound on his skull?
When the Egyptians built the tomb of Ramses VI, they covered over Tutankhamun's tomb.
Lucky Tut! The ancient grave robbers couldn't find his treasure.
Can you see anything?
Yes, wonderful things ...
When Tutankhamun's grave was opened, did a 3,300-year-old curse escape? Five months later, Lord Carnarvon was dead. Soon, over half of the 22 people closely involved with Tut's tomb also died, all of mysterious fevers or sudden blood or heart problems. Some stories link Tut's curse to 36 deaths. But Tutankhamun wasn't the only mummy reported to be cursed. A strange story is told about the mummy of Princess Amun-Ra, which was linked to 46 unusual deaths before it was sent by ship to America. The name of the ship was TITANIC.
The ancient Egyptians believed in life after death. The dead person would need his body, so it was preserved or mummified.
That's spooky. What happened to Howard Carter? Find out on page 30

A Viking Silver Hoard

Hello, hello, what's this? On May 15, 1840, an English workman stops digging to examine a strange black shape on his shovel. He picks out a small blackened disk, scrapes it with his thumbnail and gasps when he sees a glint of silver shining through.

A simple workman's shovel has just unearthed an incredible silver treasure hoard that has been hiding for about 930 years in the banks of the River Ribble at the English town of Cuerdale.

Who buried the silver and why? The clues are in the treasure itself and historians find the answers.

Blimey! This treasure is worth a fortune! It belongs in a bank.

The treasure is huge! The lead treasure chest has corroded away but the 8,600 pieces of silver just need a little polishing. There are over 7,000 silver coins and 36 kilograms (80 pounds) of silver jewelry, bars, and hacked-up silver bits, ready for the melting pot.

Now here are some clues. Most of the coins come from England's Viking territory and none are newer than the year 905. There are quite a few Viking armbands too! Have you guessed who buried the treasure?

Who buried the treasure? Hmm, let's see. I know, I'll just read the title.

Alright, alright. But read on and discover the rest of the story.

Wow! Some Vikings were not nice at all! Around 789, these men from Norway, Denmark, and Sweden sailed south and terrorized the coasts of England, Ireland, and Europe. They stole fortunes, burned villages, tortured, and killed.
NORWAY
SWEDEN
DENMARK
Dublin
Treasure!
DANELAW
Eventually many Vikings dropped their nasty ways and turned to farming and trading. They settled in England around 878 and called their territory Danelaw.
Vikings settled in Dublin, Ireland, too, but they weren't half as nice as the English Vikings. In 902, the Irish defeated the Vikings and kicked them out of Ireland. The Dublin Vikings sailed the short distance across the Irish Sea to the safety of the River Ribble and Danelaw.
Grrrr
Kill
Which brings us to the treasure. Historians think they know its story. Those exiled Vikings planned to take back Dublin. They had collected a huge war chest of silver to pay for the battle and were getting ready to sail back to Ireland, but something went wrong!
Our plans have been discovered. Hurry!
This heavy chest is slowing us down. We'll hide it in the river-bank and come back for it later.
They buried the chest in the damp banks of the River Ribble, intending, of course, to come back and get it. No one did, and the incredible Viking hoard hid for 930 years!

The A-maze-ing Pearl

On the sea floor or river bottom, a humble mollusk spins a tiny treasure inside its shell. It's a perfect pearl!

Only royalty and rich people can afford this tiny natural wonder, for perfectly round pearls are really rare. You might have to open 10,000 shells to find one!

Want to learn more about this hidden treasure? Dive into this maze and learn a few pearls of wisdom along the way.

START HERE
Mollusks and pearls have been around some 530 million years!
What's the most expensive drink in history? Egypt's Queen Cleopatra crushed and dissolved her pearl earring in a glass of wine. Then she drank it!
GULP!
Uh-oh, one of the mollusks can't spit out that itchy grit! It smooths over the problem with a thin pearly covering called nacre (NAY-ker).
Oysters, clams, and mussels—all these mollusks make pearls of different shapes and sizes.
I'm perfectly round and much more valuable than you.
Good! Maybe they'll drill a hole in you and string you up.
The nacre smooths the itch but the mollusk can't stop. It keeps adding layer after layer of the pearly stuff.
nucleus (itchy bit)

The solution is on page 30.

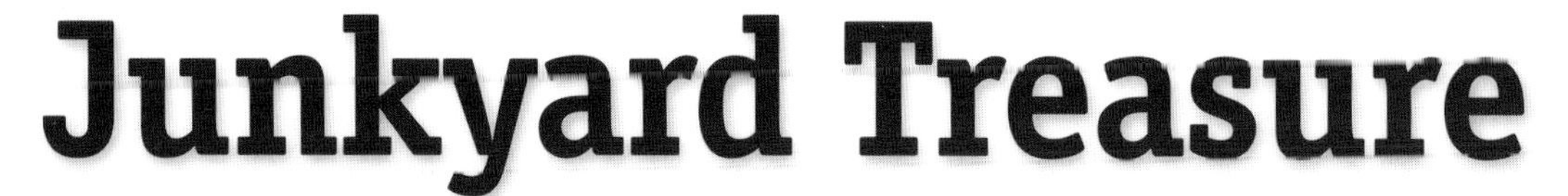

Junkyard Treasure

It's amazing what some people throw away! Deep in a New York wrecking yard, a treasure hides among the rusting engines, broken washing machines, and old plumbing pipes.

It's a Bugatti Royale. This rare and beautiful old car, one of only six, is worth a fortune!

In 1943, people see the old-fashioned car in the junkyard only as an elegant piece of scrap metal. A young man called Charles Chayne sees something else. He sees treasure!

The Bugatti Royale is big! It holds the record as the largest car ever produced.

It needs to be big. The engine was designed to pull railway trains too!

Designed and built in France by Ettore Bugatti, this majestic car was made for kings! Unfortunately, in the early 1930s, buyers were hard to find for the incredibly expensive car and only three were sold. The remaining three cars remained at the factory.

Dr. Josef Fuchs ordered his Bugatti Royale in 1932, but he and his new car were soon on the move. They left Germany, drove to Switzerland, then carried on to Shanghai in China. The last stop for the car was New York, U.S.A.

In the cold winter of 1937–38, the engine froze and cracked. Fuchs couldn't find a Bugatti Royale mechanic and the car soon became scrap-metal junk.

Can you find 20 rats in this picture? See page 30.

I wonder why the hood ornament is an elephant?
What did you expect on a big car like this, a rat?
It's more than 6.7 meters (22 feet) long! Measure any car, then compare.
The Bugatti Royale! It's beautifully made, enormously big, and incredibly rare. It's a true treasure!
Two Bugatti Royales remain in France and are registered French national treasures just like the Eiffel Tower. Another Bugatti Royale became the world's most valuable car when it sold for an incredible 15 million dollars in 1990.
Charles Chayne purchased the junkyard car for only $412 in 1943. He repaired and restored the neglected car and its engine. And don't forget the new paint!
Each Bugatti Royale is unique. No two are exactly alike!

Gold Rush!

What's going on in the Yukon, near Canada's Klondike River? There's a rumor about a gold strike in the north, but no knows a thing until a grimy ship steams into San Francisco Bay.

Townsfolk stop and stare as grubby men and women, dressed in ragged clothes, step ashore with heavy bulging bags and ask to be taken to the nearest smelting works.

That's curious! Why do they need a high-temperature furnace that separates metal from ore? Maybe those rumors of gold are true! People race to the smelting works to find out what's in those bags.

They're full of gold! Gold from the Klondike.

Two days later, another treasure ship lands in Seattle and the gold rush is on.

Gold! On August 16, 1896, George Carmack and Skookum Jim discover lots of the shiny stuff right here, near the Klondike and Yukon Rivers. Lucky people living nearby hear the news first and rush in to claim some good gold mining land.

You guessed it! The ones who strike it rich pack up their gold and sail south the following spring.

About 100,000 gold seekers rush north in 1897–98, with high hopes of getting rich. Here's one way to get to the gold—first take a steamship to Alaska then start the twisting 1000 km (620 mile) trek to the Klondike with a staggering climb up the Chilkoot Mountain Pass.

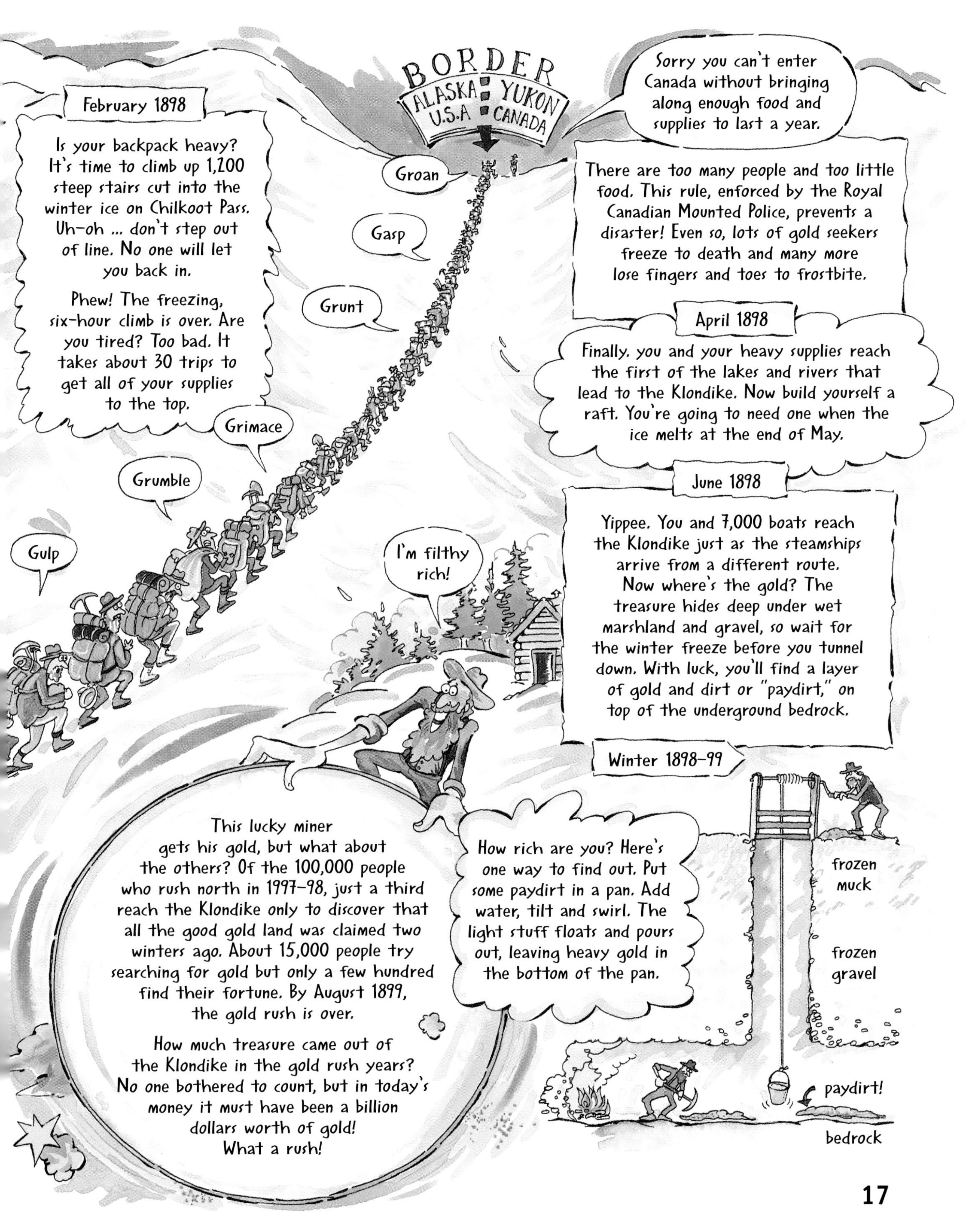
BORDER
ALASKA U.S.A
YUKON CANADA
February 1898
Is your backpack heavy? It's time to climb up 1,200 steep stairs cut into the winter ice on Chilkoot Pass. Uh-oh ... don't step out of line. No one will let you back in.
Phew! The freezing, six-hour climb is over. Are you tired? Too bad. It takes about 30 trips to get all of your supplies to the top.
Groan
Gasp
Grunt
Grimace
Grumble
Gulp
Sorry you can't enter Canada without bringing along enough food and supplies to last a year.
There are too many people and too little food. This rule, enforced by the Royal Canadian Mounted Police, prevents a disaster! Even so, lots of gold seekers freeze to death and many more lose fingers and toes to frostbite.
April 1898
Finally, you and your heavy supplies reach the first of the lakes and rivers that lead to the Klondike. Now build yourself a raft. You're going to need one when the ice melts at the end of May.
June 1898
Yippee. You and 7,000 boats reach the Klondike just as the steamships arrive from a different route. Now where's the gold? The treasure hides deep under wet marshland and gravel, so wait for the winter freeze before you tunnel down. With luck, you'll find a layer of gold and dirt or "paydirt," on top of the underground bedrock.
I'm filthy rich!
Winter 1898–99
This lucky miner gets his gold, but what about the others? Of the 100,000 people who rush north in 1997–98, just a third reach the Klondike only to discover that all the good gold land was claimed two winters ago. About 15,000 people try searching for gold but only a few hundred find their fortune. By August 1899, the gold rush is over.
How much treasure came out of the Klondike in the gold rush years? No one bothered to count, but in today's money it must have been a billion dollars worth of gold! What a rush!
How rich are you? Here's one way to find out. Put some paydirt in a pan. Add water, tilt and swirl. The light stuff floats and pours out, leaving heavy gold in the bottom of the pan.
frozen muck
frozen gravel
paydirt!
bedrock

Troy's Tale

The great walled city of Troy is no match for the ancient Greeks! They come to rescue the beautiful Queen Helen, who was kidnapped by King Priam's son, Paris, and held captive behind Troy's massive walls.

This story is over 500 years old before the poet Homer writes it down in the *Iliad* around 700 BCE.

In 1832, it is now seven-year-old Heinrich Schliemann's turn to read about the adventures at Troy. Surely this city is real. He has to find it!

When Schliemann grows up, he searches for clues in the pages of the *Iliad* and matches the description in the story with a hill called Hissarlik, near the Turkish coast of the Aegean Sea.

Now Schliemann does something that no one else has ever thought to do. He digs!

To the amazement of the world, Heinrich Schliemann finds Troy and treasure too!

START
Dig into the past and discover Troy.

Where is Troy? Schliemann searches the Iliad for clues and travels to Turkey in 1868.

This is it! The hill at Hissarlik in Turkey matches the description in the Iliad.
GO AHEAD 2 SPACES

Troy IX.	300 BCE–300 CE
Troy VIII.	1000–300 BCE
Troy VII.	1250–1000 BCE
Troy VI.	1800–1250 BCE
Troy V.	1900–1800 BCE
Troy IV.	2000–1900 BCE
Troy III.	2200–2000 BCE
Troy II.	2500–2200 BCE
Troy I.	3600–2500 BCE

Schliemann is looking for Troy VI. He finds treasure at Troy II.

The treasure is safely hidden during World War II, but when the war ends, Troy's treasure has disappeared!
GO BACK 3 SPACES

FINISH?
Wait 48 years and see what happened to the treasure.*

* Or turn to page 30

GREECE
TURKEY
Hissarlik
NORTH AFRICA
Schliemann digs without government permission in 1870 and uncovers a thick wall. Is this Troy?
MISS A TURN
OH NO! Turkish officials stop the illegal digging after only 13 days!
GO BACK 3 SPACES
Schliemann gets a digging permit in 1871, hires 100 men, and carries on!
Schliemann finds older ruins under the wall he discovered last year.
Hissarlik is like a nine-layer cake. The bottom layer is the oldest and the top layer is the freshest and newest. Yummy!
To see inside the cake, Schliemann cuts out a 40 meter (130 foot) long slice!
Yikes! Schliemann digs right through the Troy he is looking for and tosses its ruins on the rock pile!
GO BACK TO START
In 1873, Schliemann finds a beautiful stone wall. Is this King Priam's palace?
Schliemann sees a glint of gold under the wall and quickly sends the workmen away. It's treasure!
Half of the treasure belongs to Turkey, but Schliemann keeps the lot and smuggles it out of the country.
MISS A TURN
In 1874, Schliemann announces that he has found Priam's treasure. (Wrong! The treasure was buried 1,000 years before Priam was born.)
GO BACK 6 SPACES
Troy's treasure is displayed in a German museum.
GO AHEAD 2 SPACES
The treasure is incredible! Among the silver and gold drinking vessels stands a silver vase filled with 8,700 gold beads! There are 6 bracelets, 60 ear and hair ornaments, and 2 spectacular "diadem" headdresses. One of these diadems contains over 12,000 links of gold chain decorated with 4,000 flat gold shapes. Schliemann is sure that this jewelry belonged to the beautiful Helen of Troy! (Wrong again!)

Gotcha *Atocha*!

Beneath the shifting sands of the Gulf of Mexico, not far from Florida's Marquesas Keys, a Spanish treasure ship called the *Atocha* lies hidden for nearly 350 years. Stacks of silver bars snag the lines of the fishermen above, who think this is just another reef. Gold, silver, coins, and emeralds are hiding, only the width of a basketball court, under the surface of the sea.

The treasure ship set sail from Cuba on September 4, 1622, but slammed into a fierce storm within days of departure. The *Atocha* hit a reef and sank slowly, carrying a fortune in treasure down to the sea floor.

In 1970, no one knows where the *Atocha* hides, but treasure hunter Mel Fisher is looking and he's getting closer!

1970

The treasure is buried under the sand, but that's no problem! We just change the direction of the boat's powerful propeller to wash and blow the sand away.

The search boat's magnometer tells if there is metal on the sea floor! Let's check it out!

Follow the fish and find the treasure trail.

The storm of 1622 wrecked two treasure ships on the same day—the *Atocha* and the *Margarita*. The Spanish found the *Margarita*, saved much of the treasure, and wrote a report describing the location. Guess what? In 1970, Mel Fisher's friend finds this old report. Fisher has been searching in the wrong place! Now he knows where to look!

Throughout the 16th and 17th centuries, Spanish galleons sailed these seas, carrying gold, silver, and emeralds from the conquered New World of South and Central America to small but powerful Spain.

The *Atocha* didn't sink straight away after it hit a reef. It drifted with the high winds into deeper water, spilling treasure here and there. Mel Fisher tracks this treasure trail for fifteen years.
1971
Yippee! An anchor, silver coins, and some gold are discovered in shallow water.
1973
Here's a pile of silver coins and three silver bars under the sand.
Ooof! Watch out. Big Feet!
1975
This way. Five of *Atocha's* big bronze cannons are found in deeper water.
ATOCHA!
Bless you.
1980
Fisher's divers discover the *Margarita* and find some treasure too!
1985
But where is the *Atocha*? Fisher is running out of places to look. Aha! Here's another cannon.
Divers find a fortune in the sand. Emeralds! Silver coins! Gold bars! But there must be more!
It's July 20, 1985, and the magnometer shows something big below. What's hiding under the sand? It's the *Atocha* and its amazing treasure. Mel Fisher and his crew dig out the treasure pile and discover 130,000 silver coins, over 3,000 emeralds, and nearly a thousand silver bars weighing up to 45 kilograms (100 pounds) each. There are gold coins, gold bars, and more gold! The list goes on and on.
Two months later … Gotcha *Atocha*!
See if you can find 10 anchors.

Page 30 has the answer.

Oooh Ur ...

Is there treasure in the tombs of the ancient city of Ur? It's time to find out!

When archeologist Leonard Woolley discovered this royal cemetery in Iraq in 1922, he didn't immediately dig it up to see what treasure he could grab. He was more interested in discovering as much as he could about Ur and the people who once lived there.

To do this, he carefully studied the layers of Ur's ruins, sometimes using dentist's tools! Woolley did not wish to repeat the mistakes Schliemann made at Troy and destroy clues to the past.

Now, Woolley knows a lot more about Ur, including the age of this 4,500-year-old burial ground, but when he digs into the royal tombs in 1929, he finds something really shocking!

It's a death pit!

Ur's royal rulers believed in an afterlife and are buried with many beautiful objects to use in the next life.

Yikes! They wanted their servants, soldiers chariot drivers, and family members to come along too!

A fantastic gold and silver helmet, beautiful gold headdresses, and necklaces of blue lapis lazuli stones and pearls shine in the sunlight for the first time in 4,500 years. There's a golden dagger, musical instruments, and a goat nibbling a golden tree. Stones and shells decorate a banquet scene on a wooden panel. And there's more!

Ur's treasures were not only buried in the royal tombs, but also worn and held by the people in the death pits.

Ur. It's old! This beautiful walled city with palaces, temples, and ziggurat was built about 6,000 years ago by the ancient Sumerian people on the banks of the Euphrates River.
Ziggurwhat?
Ziggurat! Mud-brick pyramid mounds were built so that the earth could meet the heavens.
Oooh Ur!
Ur was abandoned over 2,000 years ago when the Euphrates River changed its route, leaving the city DRY. You can see Ur's ruins today in Iraq.
Did you hear the news? The king just died.
That's grave news for me. I'm one of his servants.
Abarji is dead! It is time for another infamous Ur funeral. As Abarji's body and his treasures are placed in the royal tomb, a procession of people calmly walk down a ramp lined with soldiers, and enter a series of pits surrounding the tomb.
Palace women wearing incredible gold and gemstone headdresses and jewelry descend into the pits, as do Abarji's senior attendants, servants, soldiers, and chariot driver. Abarji's widow, Shubad, takes her place in a chamber above her husband's tomb. They all sip a poisoned potion and calmly lie down, ready to serve their master in a new life.
Woolley discovers about 75 skeletons in Abarji's largest death pit and counts more than 600 people who sacrificed their lives for the royal rulers of Ur.

Oak Island Money Pit

Sixteen-year-old Daniel McGinnis forgets all about hunting when he sees a strange sight. An old ship's pulley, tied to a tree, dangles over a dent in the earth below.

This can only mean one thing. Something heavy was lowered into the ground with the pulley, then buried. Can it be the pirate treasure of Captain Kidd?

Daniel's discovery in 1795 begins a treasure hunt on Nova Scotia's Oak Island that lasts for more than 200 years!

They'll need pots of money to dig out this pit!
Daniel rushes off to get two friends and some shovels. The boys soon find a layer of stones covering a pit, then deeper down they discover three oak log platforms, each one 3 meters (10 feet) apart.
I'm tired and dirty.
You look pitiful. Let's take a break.
How about an eight-year break? We'll meet under this tree around 1803.

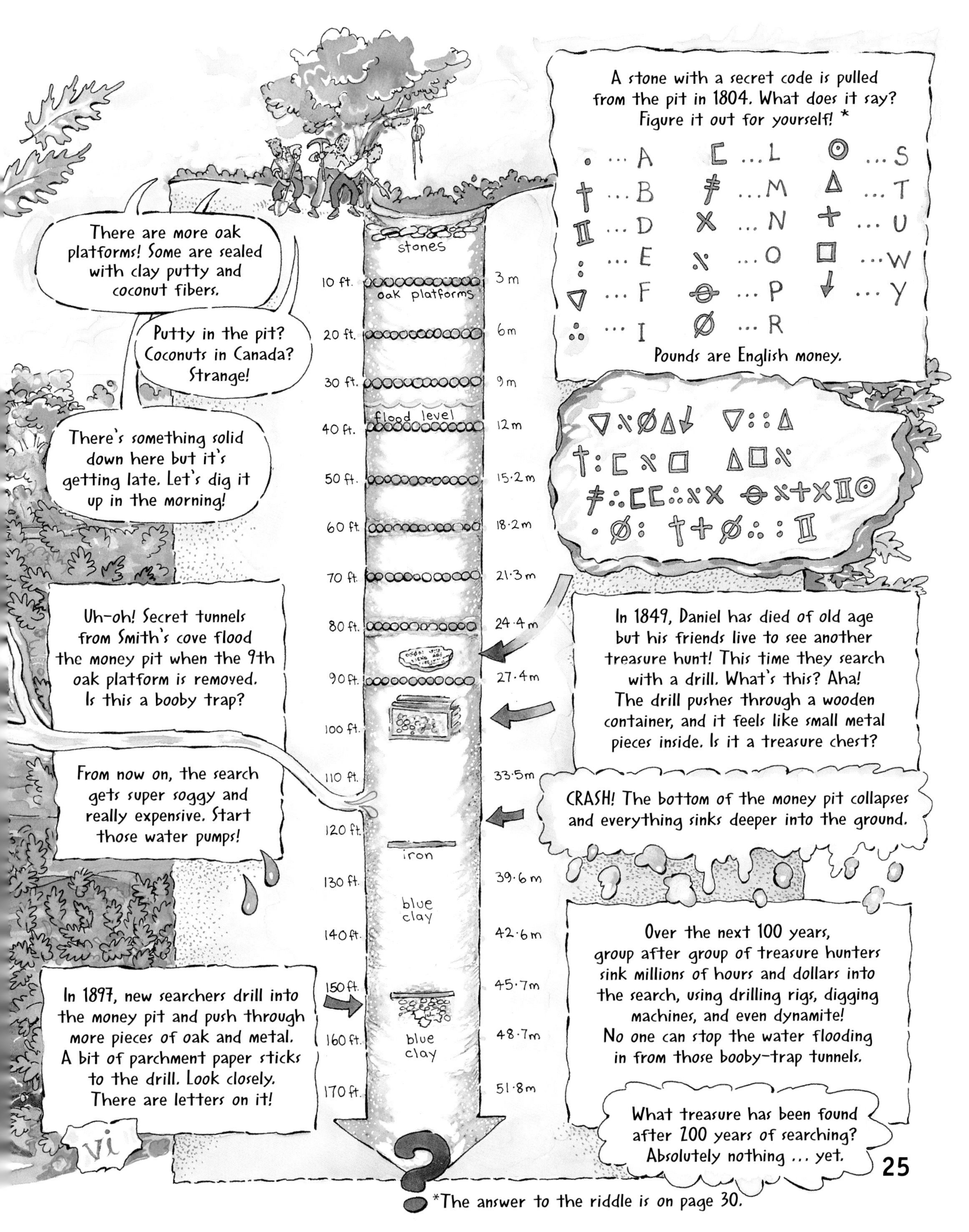

*The answer to the riddle is on page 30.

Lost and Found

It's easy to lose treasure. The stuff is so valuable that people go to a lot of trouble to hide it, bury it, or steal it.

Oops! Sometimes they lose it too. Check the notice board and discover more about treasures lost and found.

FOUND IN A FLEA MARKET!
In Pennsylvania, U.S.A., during 1989, a really rare and important document is discovered inside a four-dollar flea-market picture frame. It's an original copy of the Declaration of Independence from 1776, and it's as crisp as the day it was printed!
This truly great treasure sold at auction in the year 2000 for over 8 million dollars!
It's my ancient long-lost gym shorts! What a treasure!
Yuk! Someone lost their lunch. Here's a stinky sandwich.
LOST
Has anyone seen my gym shorts?
SCHLIEMANN FINDS MORE TREASURE!
That ancient poet Homer wrote about King Agamemnon, the brother-in-law of the beautiful Helen of Troy. This powerful king was murdered by his wife when he returned to Mycenae after his battles at Troy.
Where? Mycenae.
The amazing Schliemann finds this place in Greece, starts digging in 1876 and discovers Agamemnon's fantastic treasures of golden crowns, amazing objects, and a magnificent gold face mask!
Uh-oh! Schliemann gets it wrong again! This can't belong to Agamemnon; the treasure is about 250 years too old.
LOST AND FOUND

LOST
Where is the tomb of China's first emperor Qin who died more than 2,200 years ago?
Legends say that thousands of life-size clay soldiers guard his underground palace filled with amazing treasures, including a model map of China, with rivers and seas flowing with silver mercury. This story sounds too amazing to be true.
FOUND
While digging a well in 1974, farmers uncover a clay soldier and find Qin's long-forgotten burial site.
Archeologists carefully reveal several thousand clay soldiers and find that no two are alike! What about the underground palace? Is it full of hidden treasure? No one knows. It hasn't been dug up yet!
LOST AND FOUND AND LOST AGAIN
When buried treasure is stolen, the whole world loses a chance to learn about a piece of the past.
LOSE ANYTHING?
Australian bowerbirds love to collect little treasures to display in their nests. Is anyone missing their glass eyeball?
LOST AT SEA
Lots of lost treasure lies on the ocean floor, including that of an entire fleet of Spanish treasure ships that sank in a hurricane in 1715. In the 1950s, Kip Wagner knows he's on the right track when he finds some old coins on a Florida beach in the U.S.A. His metal detector soon discovers coins, cannonballs, and a diamond ring buried in the sand.
There must be a wreck close to shore! Wagner searches the shallow seas from an airplane and soon spots a dark shape of a ship. It's the final resting place of a ship from the lost fleet of 1715.
Sea worms have eaten away the wooden hull, but the ship's heavy ballast stones and cannons remain. Oh yes, there's treasure too, thousands and thousands of gold and silver coins. It's a fortune!
No coins are newer than the year 1715.
WHAT A FIND!
It's hard to imagine that a Roman villa once stood in a barley field at Shapwick, England. There's hardly a trace left. But buried treasure swings the dial of a metal detector when two curious cousins search the area in 1998.
What do they find? Just a few shovelsful of soil uncover 9,213 Roman silver coins that have been hiding for more than 17 centuries!

Now You Know

Don't crack that ancient tea cup! Put the shovel down and dig instead with a spoon, stick and toothbrush.

Don't hesitate to ask for help and advice from your local museum or university. Your treasure could change what we know about the history of the world!

Do you need an agreement with old Macdonald before you dig up his farm? You bet! If you dont, any treasure will belong to him instead of a reasonable 50–50 split. Ee-eye-ee-eye-oh!

Do you get to keep the treasure? It depends on where you are. Each country and sometimes each district has its own set of rules.

Maybe you'll keep 100% of your treasure if it's on private land, 50% on public land, and 0% on historically protected lands. There are lots of different laws, so you must find out which apply to you.

Don't dig a hole on a crowded beach and shout, "TREASURE." You might get trampled to death.

Do you know that the state of Florida, U.S.A., now protects the sites of those old Spanish shipwrecks that lie close to shore? How can archeologists discover a picture of the past if people keep swimming away with pieces of the puzzle?

Don't worry! Those treasure laws aren't too hard to find. Get the facts about antiquities acts from your government, museum, dive shop, or the Internet.

Do the research and discover the story behind those old ruby-red slippers. If they're Dorothy's shoes from "The Wizard of Oz," they're worth $6,000,000.00!

Do you know that smuggling treasures and artifacts in or out of a country can get you into deep trouble with the law?

Here's how to take a closer look at the treasures in this book!
M·U·S·E·U·M

Tutankhamun's Tomb (pages 8–9)

Tut's treasure suffers a little wear and tear on its world tour in the 1970s, so it's wisely decided that Tut must stay put at the Egyptian Museum in Cairo, Egypt.

A Viking Silver Hoard (pages 10–11)

Not all of these riverbank coins, (the Cuerdale Hoard), are in the British Museum in London, England; one coin apiece was given to the workmen who dug them up!

The A-maze-ing Pearl (pages 12–13)

Pearls and mother-of-pearl, (the shell's shiny lining), have survived in tombs and troves for centuries.

Junkyard Treasure (pages 14–15)

The Bugatti Royale, now painted cream, is on display in the U.S.A. at the Henry Ford Museum in Dearborn, Michigan.

Gold Rush! (pages 16–17)

Klondike gold is everywhere, maybe in your grandmother's wedding ring!

Follow the gold rush route today and hike the Chilkoot trail.

Troy's Tale (pages 18–19)

The Russians call it "Priam's Gold" and it shines in Moscow's Pushkin Museum.

Gotcha *Atocha*! (pages 20–21)

The Mel Fisher Maritime Museum in Key West, Florida, U.S.A., started its superb shipwreck collection with a $20 million treasure donation from Fisher himself.

Oooh Ur! (pages 22–23)

Gaze at Ur's grave treasure at the British Museum, London, England; the University of Pennsylvania Museum, U.S.A., and the Iraq Museum, Baghdad, Iraq.

Oak Island Money Pit (pages 24–25)

There's nothing to see! Even the stone with a secret code has vanished!

Lost and Found (pages 26–27)

Emperor Qin's life-size clay army still stands on guard near Xian, China.

Stare at Schliemann's "Mask of Agamemnon" at the National Archeological Museum in Athens, Greece.

Spend time with those Roman coins found in a farmer's field. The Shapwick Hoard is on view at the Somerset County Museum in England.

See some coins and artifacts from the lost fleet of 1715 at the McLarty Treasure Museum in Vero Beach, Florida, U.S.A.

The flea-market Declaration of Independence is in a private collection.

For the Curious

Tutankhamun's Tomb
(pages 8–9)

"Death shall come on swift wings to him who disturbs the peace of the King." It's the mummy's curse, supposedly found at Tut's tomb and the newspapers sell out quickly whenever they tell yet another shocking story to their spellbound readers. Is the curse real? If so, Carter must surely die a quick and mysterious death! Guess again. Howard Carter lives for another 17 years and dies peacefully at the age of 64.

Troy's Tale
(pages 18–19)

Troy's treasure has disappeared! What a rotten end. For 48 years, no one knows if Troy's ancient treasure was bombed, burgled, melted, or mangled!

Finally in 1993, the Russian government tells all. Troy's treasure has been safely in Moscow's Pushkin Museum since the Russian army secretly snatched it away from the defeated Germany at the end of World War II.

Solutions

The A-maze-ing Pearl
(pages 12–13)

Junkyard Treasure (pages 14–15)

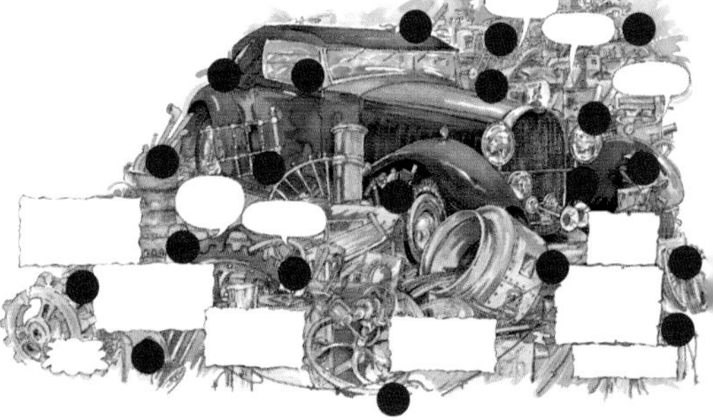

Gotcha *Atocha*!
(pages 20–21)

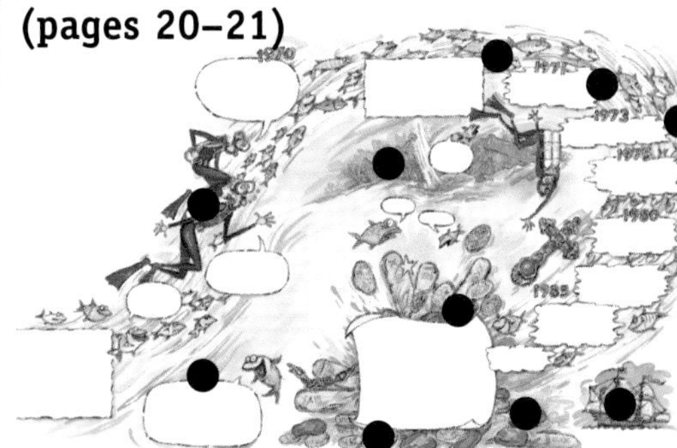

Oak Island Money Pit (pages 24–25)

Forty feet below, two million pounds are buried

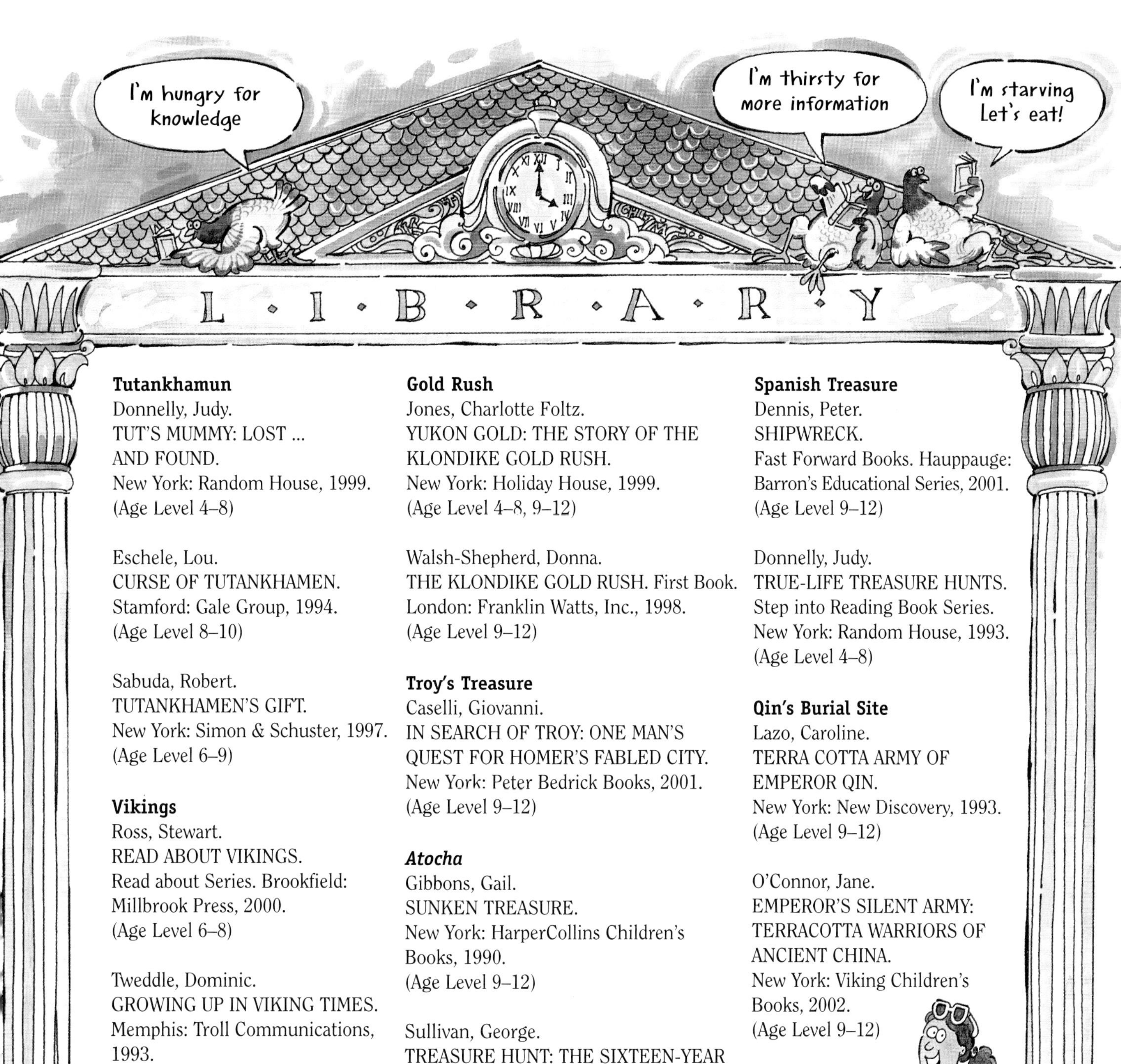

Tutankhamun
Donnelly, Judy.
TUT'S MUMMY: LOST ...
AND FOUND.
New York: Random House, 1999.
(Age Level 4–8)

Eschele, Lou.
CURSE OF TUTANKHAMEN.
Stamford: Gale Group, 1994.
(Age Level 8–10)

Sabuda, Robert.
TUTANKHAMEN'S GIFT.
New York: Simon & Schuster, 1997.
(Age Level 6–9)

Vikings
Ross, Stewart.
READ ABOUT VIKINGS.
Read about Series. Brookfield:
Millbrook Press, 2000.
(Age Level 6–8)

Tweddle, Dominic.
GROWING UP IN VIKING TIMES.
Memphis: Troll Communications,
1993.
(Age Level 8–11)

Wright, Rachel.
THE VIKING NEWS.
Cambridge: Candlewick Press, 2001.
(Age Level 9–14)

Gold Rush
Jones, Charlotte Foltz.
YUKON GOLD: THE STORY OF THE
KLONDIKE GOLD RUSH.
New York: Holiday House, 1999.
(Age Level 4–8, 9–12)

Walsh-Shepherd, Donna.
THE KLONDIKE GOLD RUSH. First Book.
London: Franklin Watts, Inc., 1998.
(Age Level 9–12)

Troy's Treasure
Caselli, Giovanni.
IN SEARCH OF TROY: ONE MAN'S
QUEST FOR HOMER'S FABLED CITY.
New York: Peter Bedrick Books, 2001.
(Age Level 9–12)

Atocha
Gibbons, Gail.
SUNKEN TREASURE.
New York: HarperCollins Children's
Books, 1990.
(Age Level 9–12)

Sullivan, George.
TREASURE HUNT: THE SIXTEEN-YEAR
SEARCH FOR THE LOST TREASURE
SHIP ATOCHA.
Hobe Sound: Florida Classics Library, 1993.
(Age Level 9–12)

Spanish Treasure
Dennis, Peter.
SHIPWRECK.
Fast Forward Books. Hauppauge:
Barron's Educational Series, 2001.
(Age Level 9–12)

Donnelly, Judy.
TRUE-LIFE TREASURE HUNTS.
Step into Reading Book Series.
New York: Random House, 1993.
(Age Level 4–8)

Qin's Burial Site
Lazo, Caroline.
TERRA COTTA ARMY OF
EMPEROR QIN.
New York: New Discovery, 1993.
(Age Level 9–12)

O'Connor, Jane.
EMPEROR'S SILENT ARMY:
TERRACOTTA WARRIORS OF
ANCIENT CHINA.
New York: Viking Children's
Books, 2002.
(Age Level 9–12)

Index

Acknowledgements

Thanks to Sheryl Shapiro, Keith and Tom Mogan, Corey Malcom, Director of Archaeology, Mel Fisher Maritime Museum, and the late Mel Fisher. —*Tina Holdcroft*